Enneagram

Learn Self Awareness, Emotional Intelligence and The 9 Personality Types of Highly Sensitive People

Table of Contents

Introduction

I want to thank you and congratulate you for purchasing the book, *"Enneagram - Learn Self Awareness, Emotional Intelligence and The 9 Personality Types of Highly Sensitive People"*.

This book contains proven steps and strategies on how to understand and make the most of your Enneagram personality type. When you understand your Ennea-type, and the Types of those around you, you begin to unlock the secrets of your potential. You can build better relationships, experience more happiness, and increase your overall wellness. This powerful tool of human psychology can put you in touch with your feelings and natural inclinations, making it easy for you to "live your best life."

In this book, you'll discover some of the driving forces behind people's actions. You'll gain insight into not only *who* people are, but *why* they are who they are, and you'll find practical suggestions on *how* to recognize when someone is under stress, then help them be their best. And when I say "someone", I also mean you! Your self-care is essential, and this book aims to help you make it easy to care for yourself, no matter what your personal goals, background, or Ennea-type.

The simple, everyday concepts and suggestions to help you manage stress, enhance your relationships, and learn from your struggles are things you can begin doing immediately, at your own pace, and in the way that works for you. Flexible and adaptable, yet proven, the Enneagram assists millions around the world every day, and I've put together this book to make it easy for you to use it, too.

Thanks again for purchasing this book. I hope you enjoy it!

Chapter One:
Enneagram Basics

What is the Enneagram?

The Enneagram of Personality is a model to understand personality types. Sometimes called a personality "test," there really is no such thing. *Tests* have right and wrong answers, whereas personality questionnaires group people who answer similarly together as a "type."

The basic Enneagram model has reportedly been used as far back as the Middle Ages, with different contributors adding to it over time. Its current form gained popularity during the 1950s, and it continues to contribute to psychological studies and discussions around the world.

The Enneagram personality model consists of a straightforward questionnaire to help determine where your personality type falls on the Enneagram figure. You use the Enneagram figure and your Ennea-type to unlock secrets to overcoming difficulties and communicate better with all types of people.

The Enneagram Figure

The figure of the Enneagram is a circle, marked with nine (9) numbered points. The nine points are connected by three overlapping, equilateral triangles, forming a harmonious, balanced symbol.

The Triads

The Enneagram personality types are organized by how people gather information and make decisions – three different "types of intelligence" based on whether the person makes decisions by listening to their *head*, their *heart*, or their *gut*.

All three types of intelligence are present in everyone, but one decision-making strategy dominates in each person.

The Head Triad (No. 5, 6, and 7)

People of Ennea-types Five, Six, and Seven are intellectual, full of ideas, and gather information to make decisions. They think things through, sometimes painfully thoroughly. People of this Triad worry about security and having "enough," which can cause them to fixate on protecting themselves by collecting knowledge.

The Heart Triad (No. 2, 3, and 4)

People of Ennea-types Two, Three, and Four tend to be attentive to what others think of them. They are emotional and sensitive, which make them prone to shame or guilt. People of this Triad overcompensate for their fears of rejection and unworthiness by adapting to new situations or people, creating a false image in order to feel love.

The Gut Triad (No. 8, 9, and 1)

People of Ennea-types Eight, Nine, and One tend to be aware of their senses and surroundings, and make decisions based on necessary, practical choices in front of them. People of this Triad can be prone to anger or aggression, which may come from having to hide their natural feelings of strength. They may overcompensate by taking on seemingly-impossible challenges in order to impact the world.

What does the figure represent?

The nine Enneagram personality types, represented by the numbers on the circle, reveal the unconscious actions and behaviors that contribute to your decisions, motivations, and unconscious coping techniques.

Depending on your answers to the questionnaire, one of these personality types is your "Main" or "Core" type. Your Core Type is connected to the two other points on the circle in its triangle, and these represent the balancing aspects of your personality.

Heart Point and Stress Point

One of the points on the triangle across from your Main Type is your "Heart Point" (aka: "Potential Point"). This is the personality type you exhibit when you feel secure and aligned; when things are going well. The natural qualities of your Heart Point's type can soften or balance the harsher aspects of your Main Ennea-type.

The other point on the triangle is your "Stress Point" (aka: "Defensive Point"), which is the personality type you exhibit when you feel overwhelmed and unable to cope; when you have exhausted your normal strategies and techniques. The natural qualities of your Stress Point's type can weaken or counterbalance the strengths of your Main Ennea-type.

Integration and Disintegration

When you are growing and at your best, when you are "reaching toward" your Heart Point, you are said to be moving in your Direction of Integration.

When you are under stress or your mental health is suffering, when you are "falling toward" your Stress Point, you are said to be moving in your Direction of Disintegration.

Other Helpful Enneagram Concepts

After you've answered the Enneagram questionnaire and know what your Main Type is, you have begun to understand yourself. While you can certainly gain a great deal by knowing only your Core Type, there are supporting concepts that allow you to take a deeper dive into the study of your personality (or someone else's!).

Wing Type

In addition to your Main Type, your results may include one of the numbers adjacent to your Main Type, known as your "Wing Type." As the name signifies, your Wing Type can *support* or *balance* your Main Type.

At times, the traits of the Wing Type may seem to conflict with the traits of your Main Type, but when you attempt to develop the best traits of your Wing Type, you can learn to balance your life.

Sub Types

Under each Main Ennea-type, there are three *Sub-Types*, which can be understood as the person's unconscious energy, the source that drives their actions and motivations. Similar to *instincts*, or *life energy*, the Sub-Type is a driving force that expresses itself through the Ennea-Type's characteristics.

Sub-Type One: Self-Preservation

The Self-Preservation Sub-Type is driven by a search for survival, comfort, and wellbeing. People of this Sub-Type are preoccupied with damage, danger, and potential exploitation, and they often focus on physical desires. Self-Preservation energy can cause a person to seek out more or grip tightly to what they have. Rather than looking outward to the group or a significant other for help with problems, they look inward for solutions.

Sub-Type Two: Social

The Social Sub-Type is driven by a search for group and community acceptance. People of this Sub-Type find safety in numbers, and they often focus on the larger group's desires. Social energy can cause a person to seek out popularity, recognition, and status, even if they must sacrifice themselves in the process. Rather than looking inward to their own thoughts or toward their significant other for solutions, they turn to the group.

Sub-Type Three: Sexual

The Sexual Sub-Type is driven by the search for intimacy and personal connection; they are sometimes said to be searching for their "other half." People of this Sub-Type find safety in a close connection, and often focus on strength and beauty, which they see as helping them to gain that safety. Sexual energy can be driven, intense, and willing to sacrifice for the relationship. Rather than looking to the group or inward to their own ideas for solutions, they turn to their closest personal relationship.

Focus of Attention

Each Ennea-type's energy will naturally gravitate either *internally* or *externally*. When internal, a person focuses their attention on their own feelings, thoughts, and impulses. When external, a person focuses their attention on other people and their environment.

Harmonic Pattern

Each Core Type handles frustration differently in an effort to achieve harmony. When your wants are frustrated, there are three main methods that you can use to handle that difficulty, and the method you gravitate toward will vary depending on your Ennea-type.

> *Types Seven, Nine, and Two* tend to handle frustration by **maintaining a positive outlook.**
> *Types One, Three, and Five* tend to handle frustration by **displaying competency.**
> *Types Four, Six, and Eight* tend to handle frustration by **reacting against it.**

Hornevian Type

Each Ennea-type addresses or resolves conflict differently. When you are confronted by a situation or a person, there are three main methods that you can use to resolve the problem, and the method you gravitate toward will vary depending on your Ennea-type.

> *Types Eight, Seven, and Three* tend to address conflict by **becoming assertive (aka: "puffing up")**.
> *Types Five, Four, and Nine* tend to address conflict by **withdrawing or hiding**.
> *Types One, Two, and Six* tend to address conflict by **complying or backing down**.

Higher Mind

When you feel whole and healthy, when you feel "awake", your Higher Mind represents the things you are capable of when you achieve a unity with your true nature. The Higher Mind stems from your essential being; it is authentic and helps you overcome stress.

Chapter Two: Ennea-Type One – "The Reformer"

Aliases: The Perfectionist, The Advocate
The Rational, Idealistic type.

Generally described as:

Principled	*Self-Controlled*
Purposeful	*Perfectionist*

At their best, Type One people are described as:

Wise	*Heroic*
Discerning	*Noble*

Motto: "I do everything the *right way*. I'm always working toward being good, making things right – isn't everyone?"

The Reformer in General

People who exhibit a Core Type One have a strong sense of right and wrong, and actively work to correct errors in themselves, others, and their world. They are conscientious and idealistic, and work to maintain high standards of fairness and equality in the world.

Reformers spend time reflecting on the consequences and outcomes of their actions. It is important to a Reformer that they don't act against their morals, even if others aren't aware of personal infractions. They are passionate, instinctive people, who direct themselves through high standards and principals.

Reformers rarely settle or roll back their expectations and are often instigators of social change, especially righting the wrongs of moral injustices. They may see themselves as being "on a mission" or having a central calling in life that directs their actions.

Sometimes, while a Type One person is working to improve something (including themselves), they can become overly critical. They greatly fear making a mistake, especially when it is seen by others, and they become impatient with themselves, others, or processes. Reformers prefer to be seen as organized, prepared, and efficient.

When a Type One person can show off as being "good" or "correct," they feel worthy and loved. A Reformer wants to be useful to their loved ones, their community, and society.

How Reformers See Themselves vs. How Others See Them

Reformers have a strong sense of purpose, but they also feel the need to justify this inner drive and their actions to others. They think they are driven by logic and reason – highly rational people – but actually Reformers operate from their inner mission and seek out reasons that explain this inner drive so others accept them.

Because Type One people are so passionate and driven, they often work to curb and control their thoughts and behaviors. While they tend to see this as "moderation" or "necessary" to keep themselves under control, it can make them seem uptight, cold, aloof, or insensitive to others. While the Type One person thinks they are keeping their cool for everyone's benefit, other people see the tight grip on self-control as constricting. At times, a Type One person may seem aggressive or resentful of their own self-control.

While the Reformer Ennea-type can see themselves as reasonably skeptical – because, in their view, the world is full of imperfections, lies, and misinformation – they can come across to others as untrusting or cold-hearted at times. The Reformer may see themselves as seeking balance between inner and outer influences, however it may appear to others that the Type One person is overly concerned and that the harmony is not achieved. While the Type One person may enjoy or seek fulfillment in the process of finding this balance, it can be frustrating or unclear to others why this process is so involved or such a priority to the Type One person.

The "Average" Reformer's Mental Health

When a Reformer is at their "average" level of mental health, they may feel regular anxiety about making mistakes and keeping reality consistent with their ideals. In this state, a Reformer may be seen as rigid by others, because they hold in feelings and become focused on work or personal projects. As they become more stressed, Reformers become nitpicky, insensitive, and emotionally reactive.

When a Reformer is feeling a little better than average, they may be dissatisfied with "everything" and begin to lecture. At this level of health, the Reformer seeks to improve the world, but can become condescending, explaining to others how things "ought" to be.

Moving Toward Integration: Reformers At Their Best

When moving in the Direction of Integration (growth) and exhibiting their best qualities, Reformers become spontaneous and joyful and can shed their anger and criticism.

Basic Desire(s): To be "good", have integrity, and be balanced

Basic Motivation(s): Desire to be "correct" and driven to improve their environment. High goals, focused on acting on personal ideals. Wants to be "right" to avoid criticism, rejection, and condemnation.

Unique Gift(s): Honest, industrious, responsible, ethical and fair. They work hard to achieve goals and visions, striving to improve the world.

Basic Goal: To embody integrity through perfection.

When Reformers Mental Health is Excellent

At their best, Reformers are wise and ready to share their wisdom. They become fluid and easy-going, less likely to emotionally react to situations.

Compassionate, inspiring, and optimistic, they share mature, well-formulated views. Their sharp eye for detail becomes a source for compliments rather than criticism.

As Type One people Disintegrate, they focus on their obligation to carry out their ideals, which can create anxiety about "perfection." Although they can find fulfillment in teaching, their personal values and perspectives on a topic can become overbearing.

Moving Toward Disintegration: Reformers When Stressed

When moving in their Direction of Disintegration (stress), the normally structured and controlled Reformer regresses toward becoming moody and irrational.

> **Basic Fear(s):** Corruption of the self, becoming "evil" or "defective"
>
> **Triggering Emotion(s):** Anger
>
> **When Fixated:** Becomes resentful

Once a Reformer becomes angry, they become defensive and treat others harshly. Because of their high ideals, the Reformer may become offended easily, and it can be difficult for them to calmly evaluate a situation. They can learn not to take things personally. When angry, Reformers push people away, which typically fuels their anger. This negative cycle can contribute to stress-related health problems, such as ulcers or high blood pressure.

What Type One People Might Struggle With

Type One people can suffer anxiety related to their efforts to make things "perfect", "correct", or "right" all the time.

At times, Type Ones can delay action until a situation or outcome is "right," causing inconveniences and delays to group productivity, if a Reformer is fixated on a detail.

They have a tendency to delay their own pleasure when focused on a project or outcome. Sometimes, this causes them to ignore or suppress their personal needs.

When Reformer's Mental Health is Struggling

When fully disintegrated and under stress, Reformers become critical enough and focused enough on punishment and "justice" that it pushes others away. They can suffer from anxiety or depression regarding their deep desire to "achieve perfection."

As Reformers begin to decrease their stress and focus on improving their health, they can become less self-righteous, increase their tolerance and patience for themselves and others, and decrease their judgmental attitudes.

Potential Addictive Struggles

Type One people might struggle with addictions to diets, including crash diets or pills, vitamins, and juice or fasting "cleanses." In some cases, a need for control can lead to eating disorders such as under-eating, anorexia, or bulimia.

Some Type One people may struggle with addictions to alcohol, in order to relieve their anxiety about the pressure to be "perfect."

Overcoming Challenges of the Reformer Ennea-Type

It's important that the Reformer take care of themselves. Relaxation, decompression, and processing their feelings, actions, and choices are essential to keeping a Type One personality balanced, healthy, and focused toward growth and integration.

Being The Best Reformer

Harness the best aspects of your Reformer Type and diminish negative traits that emerge under stress. If you're a Reformer, or know someone who is, consider how the following techniques help unlock and grow the best version of yourself.

Relaxation

Type One people need to give themselves a break. They work hard, and sometimes they forget to (or ignore the need to) let out pent-up energy and emotion. To maintain balance, a Reformer must relax as intensely as they work. It can be difficult to let go of the need for "perfection," so relaxation should be in a judgment-free environment.

Type One people can find release of their emotions through *journaling, exercise, artistic expression,* or *meditation.* When given a chance to process and express emotions, they may find the release they need. These breaks can be small, but any chance to decompress can help a Reformer feel more balanced.

Suggestions:
Focus on doing something beautiful – not "perfect." Dance. Draw. Paint. Sculpt. Knit. Write. Swim. Suntan. Meditate. Play a cooperative board or card game. Converse with a nonjudgmental friend. Exercise. Practice yoga. Find something to laugh about.

There are many simple things a Reformer can do to release their creative energy, especially when they give themselves the freedom to make mistakes without criticism.

Mentoring
Type One people naturally love to acquire and distribute knowledge, and when they do, they can have a huge influence those around them. The Reformer at their best finds joy in helping someone learn something new, and they feel bonded to people they teach.

Although a Reformer can become frustrated and impatient teaching others, learning to focus on the joy of guiding others helps a Reformer hone patience and empathy.

Suggestions:

Spend time with children and elders. Tutor. Volunteer. Babysit. Start a podcast or blog on one of your favorite topics. Join or start a Meetup or other group.

There are many simple things a Reformer can do to release their loving and educational energy, especially when they give themselves permission to laugh and learn together with others.

Chapter Three:
Ennea-Type Two –
"The Helper"

Aliases: The Giver, The Supporter
The Caring, Interpersonal type.

Generally described as:

Generous	*People-Pleasing*
Demonstrative	*Possessive*

At their best, Type Twos are described as:

Selfless	*Unconditionally Loving*
Altruistic	*Nurturing*

Motto: "I must help others. I try to be loved by loving."

The Helper in General

People who exhibit a Core Type Two have a strong desire to love and be loved, and actively work to please people around them. They place a high priority on the "good" and "true" things in life, such as love, friendship, family, and community.

Type Two people genuinely desire to help others and are concerned about being perceived as helpful.

They are often sentimental and loyal, even to the point of self-sacrifice. Helpers rarely break away from relationships without traumatically severing the bond with the person.

When a Type Two person can fully engage and express themselves, they become the caring, nurturing center for their groups of family, friends, and social circles. They enjoy caring for others during times of stress and illness, selflessly sacrificing their time and interests to ensure the people in their lives are happy, safe, and provided for. They make excellent emotional "harbors" for others in difficult times, as it is naturally easy for them to be accepting, warm, consoling, and nonjudgmental.

Sometimes, while a Type Two person is working to develop a relationship with someone, they can become possessive and jealous if the person doesn't display the same emotional intensity or commitment. They greatly fear rejection and will change themselves or ignore their needs to gain affection from others. Helpers prefer to be seen as needed – a pillar of support and a generous source of acceptance for the people they love.

When a Type Two person can develop a relationship of give-and-take with others, in which both people are mutually loving, they feel fulfilled. Their natural generosity is self-rewarding, and they receive pleasure from expressing and acting on the concern and love they have for others. Doing "good" for others makes a Helper feel worthwhile.

How Helpers See Themselves vs. How Others See Them

Helpers see themselves as genuinely invested in the best interests of others, but they can also become attached, jealous, and resentful of the time and energy they invest. They think they are driven by a true desire to be helpful – highly altruistic – but actually Helpers generally operate under pressure to do the "right thing." They often seek reassurance that they are "worthy" of love. While the Helper believes that their self-sacrifice is pure, other people may see the sacrifice as manipulative, or as a way to try to "buy" love.

Helpers are highly invested in seeing themselves as helpful, sometimes despite the feedback they receive. While they think others may not recognize it, this drive to help others and be acknowledged for it can cause Type Two people a great deal of anxiety.

Because Type Two people are so in-tune to the levels of acceptance from others, they may use self-deceptive techniques to protect their pride. They prefer to think of themselves in glowing, positive terms and can be highly sensitive to rejection. Then, some Type Two people repress or compartmentalize their personality. With too much of this, the Helper's anger can build up over time, eventually erupting in a dramatic event.

While the Helper Ennea-type can see themselves as the embodiment of loving actions – because, in their view, they always put others first – they can come across as needy or manipulative at times. The Helper can see themselves as the facilitator or manager of the relationships in their lives, however it may appear to others that the Type Two person is overly involved in other people's business. While the Type Two person may find fulfillment in caring for others, it can be frustrating to others when the Type Two person begins to pull back and direct their energies toward something else.

The "Average" Helper's Mental Health

When a Helper is at an average level of health, they feel a need to be needed. They are open and giving, but also expect a return of their outward energy, which can send confusing messages to others. Sometimes intrusive and possessive, Helpers at this level tend to exhibit some co-dependent tendencies, while also priding themselves on what they do and how helpful they are to others.

When a Helper is feeling better than average, they may be full of the best intentions for those around them, while coming across as intrusive or demanding. At this level of health, a Helper wants everyone to feel good about themselves and is quick to hand out flattery and approval of others, but they may be sensitive when people don't return their open emotional expressions.

Moving Toward Integration: Helpers At Their Best

When moving in their Direction of Integration (growth) and exhibiting their best qualities, Helpers become selfless, displaying high levels of emotional intelligence, and can shed their pride and narcissism.

Basic Desire(s): To feel loved and appreciated

Basic Motivation(s): To be loved, needed, and appreciated; to express feelings for others and elicit a response, to justify their claims about themselves.

Unique Gift(s): Generous, sensitive to others' needs and emotions, and creative with their energy, which can make them incredibly romantic. They work hard to show their support and loyalty to those they love.

Basic Goal: To connect with love through deep relationships.

Generous, considerate, and charming, a Type Two person at their best makes people feel at home. They make others feel good about themselves; they make others feel secure. They are reliable, compassionate, and above all, *helpful*. They assist, they support, and they love with respect.

When a Helper's Mental Health is Excellent

When at their best, Helpers are altruistic, giving unconditional love to themselves and others. They become unselfish and humble, recognizing the privilege they enjoy being a part of the lives of others. Compassionate, caring, and thoughtful, they embody encouragement and appreciation, and their connectivity is less needy, less absorbing of other people's energy, and becomes a source of inspiration and support for others.

As Type Two people disintegrate, they shift their connective energy with others to a more demanding interaction, which can make them "needy" or "high-maintenance." Although they enjoy and find fulfillment in helping others meet their needs, they can become demanding and resentful that they give energy to others without receiving the same levels of energy in return.

Moving Toward Disintegration: Helpers When Stressed

When moving in their Direction of Disintegration (stress), the normally nurturing and empathetic Helper regresses toward becoming dominating and self-absorbed.

> **Basic Fear(s):** Afraid of being unwanted and/or unworthy of being loved
>
> **Triggering Emotion:** Pride
>
> **Becomes Fixated On:** Flattery

Needy, manipulative, and demanding, a Type Two person under stress is imaging themselves constantly in their most terrifying truth: *they are worthless*. When a Helper feels unloved or unappreciated, they doubt their own value and to work to "win" or "earn" love from others. They expect sacrifices to be rewarded with love and appreciation, although they try to hide it. They are false and selfish, but most of all, *they need help*. When a Helper feels neither love nor respect, they are desperate for assistance and support.

What Type Two People Might Struggle With

Type Two people can suffer from emotional repression, resentment, or bitterness related to not receiving the love they feel they deserve.

At times, Type Twos can become manipulative in order to get the attention they seek and can develop different personas for different groups of people in order to "earn" love and acceptance from each. A Type Two person might spend time and energy ignoring or "pushing aside" their authentic self, to the point they feel controlled by their relationships and long for freedom from them.

Type Twos tend to overlook or ignore their own needs when seeking emotion from others. Possessiveness, jealousy, and manipulative behaviors can complicate their intense need to be loved.

When Helper's Mental Health is Struggling

When fully disintegrated and under stress, Helpers become bitter and entitled, feeling their suffering is not appreciated; they are not receiving the love they "deserve." They can suffer from emotional binge eating or addictive behaviors, to seek out the joy they aren't getting from their personal connections.

As Helpers decrease their stress and focus on their health, they become less angry and manipulative, more honest about their own motives and the motivations of others. The healthier the Helper's mindset, the less they will focus on the love they aren't receiving and begin to focus on the love they have to give.

Potential Addictive Struggles

Type Two people might struggle with addictions to food and can binge eat under stress. In some cases, feelings of being unloved or unworthy can lead to eating disorders.

Some Type Two people struggle with addictions to medications or alcohol, attempting to find pleasure in a substance instead of a person. In order to get attention and sympathy, an unhealthy Type Two person may engage in faking illnesses or exhibit hypochondria.

Overcoming Challenges of the Helper Ennea-Type

It's important that the Helper take time to take care of themselves. Self-care is essential for a Helper, because if a Type Two is not taking care of themselves, they simply can't care for others. Rest, proper diet, and loving actions toward themselves can help the Helper stay balanced and at their best.

Being The Best Helper

Harness the best aspects of your Helper Ennea-type and diminish negative traits that emerge under stress. If you're a Helper, or know someone who is, consider how the following techniques can help you unlock and grow the best version of yourself.

Practice Listening

Type Two people need to give themselves proper credit. They love deeply, and sometimes they can't recognize or accept care from others. To maintain balance, a Helper must hear and absorb other people's affections and support, and they must learn to take "no" for an answer when their help isn't needed. Helpers struggle to let go of the need for attention, so learning to listen to others may involve learning to understand other people's emotions when they don't "look" the way the Helper expects.

Type Two people find joy in listening to others' true perspectives, especially if they can use those perspectives to counteract their internal self-doubt. *Individual or group therapy* can teach a Type Two to actively engage with others' communication styles. In particular, studying people's *"Love Languages"* can really sharpen a Helper's empathy and ability to connect.

Suggestions:

Focus on doing something quiet – to hear other languages. Listen to international music or nature sounds (rain, ocean shores, bird songs, etc.). Listen to a podcast or nonfiction audio book, especially something motivational or comical. Practice yoga or meditation. Study and apply knowledge of the Love Languages.

There are simple things a Helper can do to hone their ability to hear and connect with positivity in themselves, especially when they give themselves freedom from the pressure to "fix the situation" for the person they're listening to.

Practice Clear Communication

Type Two people naturally love to communicate, and when they refine these skills, they make huge impacts on the people around them. The Helper at their best finds joy in clearly demonstrating and expressing their love. They are fulfilled when other people acknowledge their caring words and actions.

Although a Helper can become frustrated when trying to express themselves, learning to choose their words to connect with others in a way they understand will help the Helper increase their feelings of social love and acceptance.

Suggestions:

Study a new language – learn words and phrases people respond to. Become aware of your motivations and practice directing your energy. Express your expectations and disappointments, without becoming emotional. When a job is done, congratulate yourself, then release other people from any "obligation" to acknowledge you.

There are simple things a Helper can do to release their thoughtful, intuitive, nurturing energy, especially when they give themselves permission to be themselves.

Chapter Four:
Ennea-Type Three –
"The Achiever"

Aliases: The Performer, The Motivator
The Pragmatic, Success-Oriented type.

Generally described as:

Adaptable	*Outstanding*
Image-Conscious	*Driven*

At their best, Type Three people are described as:

Authentic	*Role Model*
Enthusiastic	*Inspirational*

Motto: "I need to succeed. Get to the top and look good doing it!"

The Achiever in General

People who exhibit a Core Type Three have a strong desire to look good to other people, because they are motivated by gaining love and acceptance through their achievements and performance. They strive to be outstanding – to *stand out*.

Type Three people genuinely want the approval and admiration of those around them, and they pour their energy into performing to others' satisfaction.

They are graceful and gracious, and easily accomplish things that others admire. Achievers sometimes equate their self-worth with their performance, and can defer to others' desires, ultimately repressing or deceiving themselves about their true wants.

When a Type Three person can fully engage and express themselves, they become shining stars; they light up any room. They enjoy inspiring and lifting others, pushing themselves and those around them to new limits. They make charming company, excellent hosts and social mediators, and become a positive force, pushing others to achieve their own hopes and dreams.

Sometimes, while a Type Three person works toward their goals, they can become single-minded and cut-throat, even disregarding the harm they do others. They greatly fear failure and rejection and work both to be successful and to seem successful. Achievers prefer to be seen as "winners," thinking of themselves as "the best" at whatever they set their minds to. This can make them open to connecting with others they see as winners, or it can make them competitive and closed off from relationships with others who can steal their spotlight.

When a Type Three person develops their social status and reputation to the extent that they receive the attention and encouragement they crave, they feel fulfilled. Type Three people are satisfied by appreciation, not the material "things" associated with success. Being seen as a star makes an Achiever feel worthwhile, which in turn drives them to encourage others to shine.

How Achievers See Themselves vs. How Others See Them

Achievers see themselves as true leaders, modeling the road to success for others to follow, but they can become narrow-minded, intense, and relentless in their pursuits. They think they are driven by a true desire to stand out – highly exceptional – but actually, Achievers generally operate under fears of being ordinary, bored, and rejected. They seek reassurance from others that their efforts and actions make them special. While the Achiever believes they are competent and deserve praise, other people may see their confidence as arrogance or snobbery.

Achievers are highly invested in seeing themselves as *worthy* – worthy of love, of admiration, of praise, of followers –

sometimes despite their competitive nature, which can push others away. When they think others don't recognize their achievements, they may work harder and perform more dramatically.

Because Type Three people are so in-tune with the wants, needs, and preferences of others, they may resort to dishonesty to boost their reputation. They prefer to think of themselves as deeply empathetic, but others may see Achievers as insensitive. While they notice and can react to other people's emotions, they don't spend much time in their own emotional landscape. When they ignore their own feelings for too long, they have trouble connecting with their true desires. This disconnect can make them angry, which they may redirect to people close to them, blaming others for "making" them work so hard.

The "Average" Achiever's Mental Health

When an Achiever is at an average level of health, they may feel naturally self-conscious and adjust themselves to meet others' expectations. They will be efficient in solving problems, thinking them through, but can lose their true desires in the process. Sometimes demanding and overbearing, Achievers at this level tend to "act out" for attention, while also downplaying their dramatic nature and single-mindedness.

When an Achiever feels a little better, they may be performing well and achieving their goals regularly, which fuels their drive to push themselves further. At this level of health, an Achiever wants to be recognized and works hard to earn that recognition, although others may become frustrated by their focus and drive.

Moving Toward Integration: Achievers At Their Best

When moving in their Direction of Integration (growth) and exhibiting their best qualities, Achievers become supportive and enthusiastic for others' achievements. As they achieve, they become less vain and self-centered.

> **Basic Desire(s):** To feel valuable and worthwhile.
> **Basic Motivation(s):** To be affirmed and recognized, to be distinguished from others and admired, and to impress others.
> **Unique Gift(s):** Positive, confident, and optimistic; always able to see the glass as half-full.
> **Basic Goal:** To be successful, productive, and accepted.

When Achiever's Mental Health is Excellent

When at their best, Achievers are genuinely generous, charming, and warmly inclusive. They can channel their drive to succeed into support for others and enjoy the accomplishments of people they support. Motivating to others, confident and caring, Type Three people embody an easy, graceful way of living that laughs loud and often. When motivated by their own achievements, they naturally elevate those around them.

As Type Three people Disintegrate, they become focused on being liked and accepted and less inclined to rely on their inner sources of confidence. Seeking the approval and acknowledgement of the group, they begin to disregard the feelings of people close to them, as they become more self-centered in their focus on achieving.

Moving Toward Disintegration: Achievers When Stressed

When moving in their Direction of Disintegration (stress), the normally ambitious and confident Achiever regresses toward becoming competitive and self-centered.

> **Basic Fear(s):** Afraid of rejection, failure, and social outcast.
> **Triggering Emotion:** Deceit
> **Becomes Fixated On:** Vanity

Outwardly focused Type Three people become apathetic and defensive under stress. Confused about their true feelings, or afraid to admit them for fear of "disappointing" others, Achievers fall prey to their self-doubts when they feel ignored. They can begin to lie to themselves and others about what they really want, and they become needy, potentially manipulative or vengeful. Most of all, they cry out for positive attention. When an Achiever can't receive recognition for their successes, they will settle for whatever gets them attention.

What Type Three People Might Struggle With

Type Three people suffer from suppressing emotions, setting aside their true desires to align with the goals of the group. Disconnecting from their authentic wants can make them lonely, even in the middle of a crowd.

At times, Type Threes can become dramatic in their search for attention, or competitive as they become frustrated when they see achievements they believe they deserve being earned by others. A Type Three person might struggle with showing their support or genuinely celebrating other people's victories, although they expect others to congratulate them on their accomplishments.

Type Threes tend to push themselves to their physical, mental, and emotional breaking points. Their expectations of themselves are high, and they can be relentlessly critical of themselves in their pursuit of excellence.

When Achiever's Mental Health is Struggling

When fully disintegrated and under stress, Achievers become vengeful, merciless in the pursuit of their goals. They can fixate on their jealousy of others' successes, even working to undermine that success. The Achiever might even excuse their insensitive actions toward others as "the ends justify the means," because they are so intensely driven to reach those ends.

As Achievers decrease their stress and focus on their health, they can reveal their inner vulnerabilities – fear of failure and humiliation. The healthy Achiever's mindset recognizes that working collectively is a path to success that can fulfill them, giving them joy they can't experience through achievements earned alone.

Potential Addictive Struggles

Type Three people might struggle with addictions associated with their ideas of success. An Achiever whose goals are physical can overwork or overstress their body, exhausting or injuring themselves and placing their physical health at risk. An Achiever whose success is defined by their professional work may overwork themselves with heavy job responsibilities, long hours, and minimal breaks or recovery time.

Some Type Three people may struggle with addictions to substances that "fuel" their desires to work long hours, push their body physically, or give off the appearance of a successful lifestyle. Caffeine, amphetamines, cocaine, steroids, or other stimulants are common addictive struggles for Achievers.

Overcoming Challenges of the Achiever Ennea-Type

Achievers must give themselves time to recharge. Honestly connecting with their inner needs is essential, because they may spend so much time performing for others that they forget themselves. Practicing self-appreciation, integrating small breaks into the day, and genuinely connecting with others helps the Achiever stay balanced and at their best.

Being the Best Achiever

Harness the best aspects of your Achiever Ennea-type and diminish negative traits that emerge under stress. If you're an Achiever, or know someone who is, consider using the following techniques to help you unlock and grow the best version of yourself.

Truthful Reflection

Type Three people need to "stop and smell the roses." They are focused and driven, and they can drive themselves to exhaustion. To maintain balance, an Achiever can take a short break – even a few deep breaths can do it – to pause during busy or stressful times. Use these moments to reconnect with true inner desires, which tend to get lost during the bustle of impressing others. Achievers can have difficulty letting go of their goals, but learning to congratulate themselves on small achievements can realign an Achiever with their next goal.

Suggestions:

Goal-oriented journaling. Meditate. Practice yoga. Keep a success chart. Scrapbooking. Garden. Bake. Clean. Keep a "To-Do" list and update when items are completed.

Develop Social Bonds

Type Three people naturally love to be around others, and when they refine their communication and bonding skills, they encourage everyone around them to achieve. The Achiever at their best finds joy in projects that don't advance them toward their own goals, but instead support the goals of others. Enhancing cooperative abilities can establish the Achiever as an appreciated, beloved leader in their community.

Achievers can become frustrated when it seems that others aren't as dedicated to the project, or when they believe they're not receiving appropriate recognition. Learning to take pride in themselves, and express their pride in others' achievements, will help the Achiever feel loved and fulfilled.

Suggestions

Take on a mentoring or teaching role. Converse with a nonjudgmental, supportive friend. Start a podcast or blog. Join an online or offline community of like-minded people. Practice active listening. Choose one time each day to contact someone you know and tell them you appreciate them. Say "thank you" at the end of every conversation.

There are simple things an Achiever can do to release their deep appreciation for talent, beauty, and leadership, especially when they give themselves permission to praise themselves and others.

Chapter Five:
Ennea-Type Four –
"The Individualist"

Aliases: The Tragic-Romantic. The Artist.
The Sensitive, Withdrawn Type.

Generally described as:

Expressive	*Self-Absorbed*
Dramatic	*Temperamental*

At their best, Type Fours are described as:

Inspired	*Transformative*
Imaginative	*Nostalgic*

Motto: "I am unique. I'm the only person who feels this way, and no one else can really understand."

The Individualist in General

People who exhibit a Core Type Four have a strong desire to feel unique and special, and actively work to distinguish themselves from others. They place a priority on discovering their "true selves" and being "satisfied with life." Type Four people genuinely desire to experience what life has to offer and are concerned about being perceived as *individuals*.

They often experience intense emotional highs and lows, even to the point of their emotions being expressed in raw, unfiltered form. Individualists long for a life of meaning, which they may see as lying in the past or future. By focusing on their fantasies, they may eventually disconnect from the people in their present.

When a Type Four person can fully engage and express themselves, they inspire and lead others. They will enjoy exploring both the dark and joyful aspects of life, relishing the emotional honesty and their attempts to convey their feelings to others. They make excellent, empathetic listeners who can give friends and loved ones a fresh perspective and insight into creative solutions, as it is natural for them to ask questions, seek reactions, and support others' individual growth.

Sometimes, while a Type Four person works to get to know someone, they are reserved, hesitant to show the vulnerabilities of their true emotions. They greatly fear being ordinary or misunderstood, and being rejected, so they may shut out others until they feel their individuality will be accepted. Individualists prefer to be seen as mysterious, rare, genuine people who will never really be understood.

When a Type Four person develops their identity to the point where they feel secure in expressing it wholeheartedly, they feel fulfilled. With a natural quiet strength, they can objectively evaluate their emotions and behaviors and adjust to align with who they "really are inside." They receive immense pleasure from recognizing uniqueness in others, and praising truth, beauty, and depth of emotion in others' creations.

How Individualists See Themselves vs. How Others See Them

Individualists see themselves as talented and special, set apart from other people. However, this self-appreciation can come across as rude, arrogant, or judgmental. While their attitude tends to isolate them, they crave attention and acceptance, because what good is it to be unique, if no one sees it? They think they are driven by a true desire to stand out – to be one-of-a-kind – but actually, Individualists generally operate from deep fear of being alone. Although the Individualist believes that their individualism is a gift, it also often acts as their own curse.

Individualists are invested in interpersonal relationships. They care about the feedback they receive from others and are sensitive and self-conscious. Although they can feel like social outcasts, or at least, socially awkward, they are also driven by feelings of love and can be incredibly romantic. They long for ideals – of time, of place, and of relationships – and nurture this desire internally while imposing their ideals on the outside world.

Because Type Fours are inclined to view themselves at outsiders, acceptance and generosity may surprise them. It may take an Individualist time to "warm up" to relationships, but once they bond with someone, they can become as invested in that person as themselves. Individualists can be prone to jealousy, which causes them to withdraw from someone they envy. They may criticize others to try to cover their disappointment in themselves. Although unable to express it, they often long to live with the ease and comfort they see in others – free from emotional pressures.

While the Individualist Ennea-type can see themselves as the embodiment of free agency and self-expression, they can come across to others as insensitive, critical, aloof, or petty. The Individualist can see themselves as nurturing the beauty within themselves, but others may see the Individualist as "acting ugly" or "weird."

The "Average" Individualist's Mental Health

When an Individualist is at an average level of health, they may engage actively in the world, then regularly withdraw to an interior world to process events and feelings. They are sensitive and creative, intuitive and imaginative, but can become protective of feelings, fighting to contain them, hiding them from others. Sometimes seen as shy and moody, Individualists can be "aloof" and hypersensitive at the same time.

When an Individualist feels better than average, they may romanticize life and become nostalgic, dreaming of the past or future. At this level, an Individualist wants to create and grow an interesting and beautiful world around themselves, because they feel passions and observations they are driven to express. Although they desperately desire to bloom, they are self-conscious and deeply afraid of others' criticism.

Moving Toward Integration: Individualists At Their Best

When moving in their Direction of Integration (growth) and exhibiting their best qualities, Individualists become calm and objective, able to shed their jealousy and emotional baggage.

Basic Desire(s): To express their genuine creativity and unique perspective; to create a satisfying, authentic identity.

Basic Motivation(s): To feel, create, and express their inner beauty. Driven to be seen as unique, and to attract special attention.

Unique Gift(s): Experience intense emotions, which they attempt to use to connect with others. Imaginative and wild, they work to make the world a better, more beautiful place.

Basic Goal: Become authentic through personal expression.

Honest, objective, and empathetic, Type Four people at their best are not afraid to look at their flaws and reveal their vulnerabilities. They make others comfortable and uplift them with a spirit of whimsy and acceptance. They are open-minded, soft-hearted, and above all *truly unlike anyone else*. They inspire, motivate, and love wholeheartedly.

When Individualist's Mental Health is Excellent

When at their best, Individualists inspire. They refuel their own creative energy through personal expression, becoming more energized with every creation or idea. Deeply curious, they seek the truth in themselves and spend their energy analyzing and interpreting how they feel about their experiences. Once they find value in the world and can express it, the results transform people.

As Type Four people Disintegrate, they shift their introspective energy to a more self-centered, even rebellious, mindset. Self-conscious and aware of others' reactions to their emotional expressions, Type Four people become mocking and judgmental, or may sink into melancholy or depression, as they seek to hide their underlying vulnerabilities.

Moving Toward Disintegration: Individualists When Stressed

When moving in their Direction of Disintegration (stress), the normally whimsical and independent Individualist regresses, becoming highly needy or disconnected and aloof.

> **Basic Fear(s):** Afraid of not establishing an authentic identity and value.
> **Triggering Emotion(s):** Jealousy
> **When Fixated:** Melancholy

What Type Four People Might Struggle With
Type Four people can suffer from depression, self-pity, and anxiety related to frustrated feelings or a sense of disconnect.

Individualists can become self-indulgent and nostalgic, wishing for their fantasies to come true. They can develop an ideal self-image that isn't aligned with the way they act, and they can lie to protect themselves from feeling inadequate or boring. They might spend time and energy convincing others that they are flawed or pitiful, while expecting the other person to try to convince them otherwise.

Type Fours tend to exaggerate, both the pleasurable and the painful, both the darkness and the light. The need to be loved and appreciated can both fuel them to push themselves further and complicate their intense desire not to be judged.

When Individualist's Mental Health is Struggling

When fully disintegrated and under stress, Individualists can feel hopeless, in despair, and trapped under the weight of their experiences and emotions. When unable to genuinely express themselves or losing connections with others, Type Four people wade through feelings of shame, exhaustion, and self-reproach, which can be a dangerous self-perpetuating cycle.

As Individuals decrease their stress and focus on higher levels of health, they become more forgiving and hopeful. Although Type Four people seek independence, they also crave connection, and experiences that result in strong emotional reactions help the Individualist maintain a healthy, positive mindset.

Potential Addictive Struggles

Type Four people might struggle with over and under-indulgent behaviors, depending on their moods and company. They can seek to fill emotional holes with food, tobacco, alcohol, or drugs, or they can seek to control emotions through self-imposed regulations on any of these.

Some Type Fours might struggle with a lack of physical activity – rather than an addiction to the physical results of exercise, the tendency toward depression makes some Type Fours lethargic and avoidant of exercise. However, the endorphin release and other endocrine effects of exercise can be successful at counteracting some types of depression.

Overcoming Challenges of the Individualist Ennea-Type

It's important that the Individualist take time to get outside their own head. Connecting with others is essential, because if a Type Four personality does not receive feedback from the outside world, they turn inside to feed their need for attention. Conversation, cooperation, and participation in something greater than themselves help them see their place in their community, keeping them balanced and at their best.

Being the Best Individualist

Harness the best aspects of your Individualist Ennea-type and diminish negative traits that emerge under stress. If you're an Individualist, or know someone who is, consider how the following techniques help you unlock and grow the best version of yourself.

Focus on the Positive

Type Four people need to keep their imaginations in check. Deep feelings and creativity can run wild, and they may have to work to dismiss feelings of negativity and reatain positive emotions. By learning to objectively evaluate feelings, rather than be caught in the turmoil of experiencing them, Individualists learn that feelings do not define them. Individualists have difficulty pulling themselves out of an emotional "funk," but positive feelings from connections with others help Individualists remember their own worth.

Type Four people can find joy in creating a routine and scheduling time to reflect, process, and evaluate their emotions and experiences. Expressing gratitude helps Individualists feel more connected to others. *Journaling, meditation,* and *artistic endeavors* can teach a Type Four to explore their feelings actively, then set them aside and move forward into new experiences.

Suggestions:

Schedule a daily routine for reflection or a small act of gratitude. Journal. Scrapbook. Paint. Meditate. Practice yoga. Listen to nature sounds or rhythmic beats to relax and release pent-up emotions. Read or listen to poetry. Sketch. Focus on positive emotions, achievements, and love and connection. Spend time with animals or children.

Turn Visualizations into Actions

Although Type Four people can imagine the future they want, they may not put forth the effort into achieving it. Type Four people naturally love to dream, but they may put off acting on their dreams until the time or the mood "is right." The Individualist at their best finds joy in creation and is fulfilled when sharing their thoughts with the world.

Commitment, discipline, and routine help an Individualist not only produce the creations that fuel their individuality, but the structure can give them the freedom to release their emotions in a controlled, practiced way.

Suggestions:

Create a routine for creativity. Schedule time to create with others. Set deadlines on projects and seek accountability from nonjudgmental friends and family. Involve yourself in a mentoring or teaching role. When others don't acknowledge you the way you want, practice not taking it personally.

There are simple things that an Individualist can do to release their inspiring, supportive energy, especially when they give themselves permission to focus their feelings into creative release.

Chapter Six:

Ennea-Type Five –

"The Investigator"

Aliases: The Observer, The Scholar, The Thinker
The Intense, Cerebral type

Generally described as:

Perceptive	*Secretive*
Innovative	*Isolated*

At their best, Type Fives are described as:

Pioneers	*Insightful*
Visionaries	*Inspiring*

Motto: "I need to understand everything. The more I know, the safer and more likeable I'll be."

The Investigator in General

People who exhibit a Core Type Five have a strong desire to know as much as possible, and actively work to think deeply about concepts and possibilities. They place priority on curiosity and developing complex ideas and skills, and they value having something insightful and useful to contribute. Type Fives genuinely desire to be known for "having ideas" and being "independent thinkers."

They are dedicated to the topics they find interesting, which can become such single-minded focus that they lose connections with others. Investigators rarely explore popular or common topics, preferring instead to push the limits of knowledge at the boundaries, and because of their niche interests, can have difficulty finding others who share those interests.

When a Type Five person can fully engage and express themselves, they are inspiring, independent, and fascinating experts in their chosen set of topics. They enjoy sharing their unique, vast knowledge with anyone interested, but if no one is interested, they can become lost in their world of ideas. They make excellent sources of creative and innovative solutions, as it is naturally easy for them to apply knowledge and different perspective to new situations.

Sometimes, while Type Five people work to discover and develop ideas, they become protective of their privacy. Secretive, fearful of others misunderstanding and seeing them as inadequate, they hide their feelings, ideas, and thoughts. They can separate people in different areas of their lives, compartmentalizing their life to protect feelings and created identity. Investigators prefer to be seen as the "go-to" person on a topic and can detach from people or avoid situations that make them feel uncomfortable or incompetent.

When a Type Five person develops healthy relationships with others and feel respected for their expertise while learning from others' experiences, they feel fulfilled. For a Type Five, "a day without learning is like a day without sunshine." Their naturally inquisitive nature rewards them. They receive pleasure from not only "knowing things" but being able to expand on the ideas of others and contribute to the collective knowledge on a subject. Impressing others with ideas makes an Investigator feel worthwhile.

How Investigators See Themselves vs. How Others See Them

Investigators see themselves as genuinely invested in the progress of knowledge and the discovery of "truth", but they can also be detached, isolated, defensive, and judgmental. They think they are driven by a true desire to be seen as competent and capable, but actually, Investigators generally operate from deep insecurity and fear of being insufficient. They often seek validation from others, although they simultaneously reject this validation, which can become a self-defeating cycle where the Investigator feels trapped in a sense of inadequacy.

Investigators are invested in seeing themselves as innovative, sometimes despite the obsessions that result. While they desperately desire that others accept their ideas and discoveries, they may become insecure if those ideas are quickly and readily accepted.

Because Type Five people are so committed to exploring "big ideas," they can see practical, everyday problems as distractions from their larger mission. This can lead to Type Five people ignoring their basic needs and social obligations, or the emotional requirements of relationships. The irony is that the more an Investigator dedicates themselves to the study of a topic, the less they can care for their practical problems, which feeds their insecurities about being capable of functioning in the world.

While the Investigator Ennea-type can see themselves as the embodiment of progress – because, in their view, they always work to "better" humankind – they can come across as closed-off, focused on strange or irrelevant topics, eccentric, or out-of-touch with reality. The Investigator can see themselves as an instrument of innovation, but it may appear to others that they are actually disconnected from people and real-world problems of day-to-day life. While Type Fives may find fulfillment in collecting and demonstrating their knowledge, it can be frustrating to others when the ideas are too complex or narrowly focused to be practical.

The "Average" Investigator's Mental Health

When an Investigator is at an average level of mental health, they may feel deeply in-tune with interesting subjects, able to apply the information to new situations. They are curious and intense, which can make them narrow-mindedly focus on rare or niche topics. Sometimes argumentative, Investigators at this level are determined to show that they know what they're talking about and their knowledge is valuable.

When an Investigator feels better than average, they may be full of joy and enthusiastic to share their new knowledge, sometimes imposing or intruding on others. They come to decisions after long deliberation but act efficiently once they reach a decision. Healthy Investigators want everyone to appreciate the love of learning for itself, as well as practically apply knowledge in fun, creative ways. However, they may become fascinated by subjects that don't resonate with the people in their lives or their community.

Moving Toward Integration: Investigators At Their Best

When moving in their Direction of Integration (growth) and exhibiting their best qualities, Investigators become confident problem-solvers and decision-makers, focused on teaching and helping others, and are able to shed their defensive self-centeredness.

> **Basic Desire(s):** To be capable, competent, dependable.
>
> **Basic Motivation(s):** To "understand everything," to "collect" knowledge, to solve problems, and to be useful. They work hard to show their ideas as worthy and valuable.
>
> **Unique Gift(s):** Knowledgeable, respectful, mental clarity, reliable, thoughtful.
>
> **Basic Goal:** To arm themselves with knowledge ("know everything") in order to defend against change, uncertainty, or environmental threats.

When Investigator's Mental Health is Excellent

When at their best, Investigators are capable, competent, and perceptive. They become not only curious, but flexible in their perspective, able to see both the "big picture" and the "small details." Pushed to discover, driven to explore ideas and question established topics, they embody natural curiosity and pioneering spirit. Their high level of energy for collecting and harvesting knowledge, combined with their attention to detail, make them a formidable force in any area of expertise.

As Type Five people Disintegrate, they shift their focus and appreciation for mastery away from people "in front of them" and toward more "distant" people and ideas. They can withdraw, applying their mental edge to something inside themselves, sharpening their ideas until they feel they are "presentable" and "worthy" of being shown to others.

Moving Toward Disintegration: Investigators When Stressed

When moving in their Direction of Disintegration (stress), the normally inquisitive and focused Investigator regresses toward becoming idiosyncratic, disorganized, even frantic.

Basic Fear(s): Worthlessness, uselessness, incompetence.
Triggering Emotion(s): Greed
When Fixated: Become secretive, withdrawn, stingy.

What Type Five People Might Struggle With

Type Five people suffer from preoccupations and obsessions with impractical, esoteric, or unnecessary ideas. This can contribute to a sense of isolation, and although they are desperate to connect with others, their limited focus on intellectual connection can prevent them from seeing the importance of physical and emotional connections.

At times, Type Fives can become narcissistic, judgmental, intense, and even nihilistic. In order to establish themselves as "smarter" than others, they can become critical of other people's ideas, attitudes, and ignorance. A Type Five person might spend such immense amounts of time and energy in a specific topic that they ignore or disregard the importance of topics that resonate with others.

Type Fives tend to let their imaginations run wild and ignore the world's pressures as they escape into fantasy and idealism. Relentless pursuit of their own identity through knowledge can both make them feel safe and vulnerable at the same time. If they cannot be safe in their minds, they often cannot find safety in others, and so have difficulty trusting people, although they intensely wish to appear trustworthy and reliable.

When Investigator's Mental Health is Struggling
When fully disintegrated and under stress, Investigators become obsessed with their ideas and inner realities. They can withdraw fully, becoming reclusive and eccentric, and even

engaging in self-harm or self-destructive behaviors. Fearful and self-absorbed, they reject relationships in favor of worlds they construct in their minds.

As Investigators decrease their stress and focus on their health, they become more attached to others and accepting of limitations in themselves and others. The healthier an Investigator's mindset, the more they can free themselves from their self-imposed restrictions and expectations and express their loving and compassionate nature.

Potential Addictive Struggles

Type Five people might struggle with poor hygiene and self-care habits, as they can neglect their health, nutrition, and physical needs when engaged in their passion. In some cases, extreme reclusive habits cause them to be hazardous to their own health.

Some Type Five people might struggle to addictions or dependencies on hallucinogens, alcohol, or prescription medications to escape anxiety related to the pressure to "know it all," or to expand their experience.

Overcoming Challenges of the Investigator Ennea-Type

It's important that the Investigator establish their own identity and cultivate an area of expertise, because if a Type Five cannot find value in their own intellect, they regress to a sense of purposelessness and meaninglessness in "everything." Rest, empathy, creative connection with their emotions, and the chance to present themselves as role models can help the Investigator stay balanced and at their best.

Being the Best Investigator

Harness the best aspects of your Investigator Ennea-type and diminish negative traits that emerge under stress. If you're an Investigator, or know someone who is, consider using the following techniques to help unlock and grow the best version of yourself.

Mind Your Mind

Type Five people need to be self-aware of their emotions and needs. They see possibilities but can become paralyzed by the need to make decisions, retreating into the world of their ideas for security. To maintain balance, an Investigator must recognize when they're ignoring or retreating from their physical and emotional needs, then push themselves to reach out to others for comfort. Investigators can have difficulty letting go of their "need to know," so learning to ask for help presents them with challenges. They must recognize that they *can't* know everything and that there are other things as important as knowledge.

Type Five people find joy in relaxation, reflection, and learning from perspectives that they aren't regularly exposed to. They may not cognitively enjoy, but will emotionally benefit from, being pulled out of their internal world to engage "in the now." They can also learn how to focus their involved decision-making process toward everyday tasks by learning to place priority on their needs and emotions.

Suggestions:

Meditate. Practice yoga. Build confidence by practicing making small, practical decisions and small, significant achievements. Use a daily to-do list to monitor emotions and activities that are focused on non-intellectual pursuits. Walk in nature. Read or write poetry. Draw. Paint. Dance.

Focus Nervous Energy

Type Five people naturally love to share what they learn, and they want others to be excited about learning. When they refine their skills to teach, they have huge impacts on those around them. The Investigator at their best finds joy in educating, instructing, and helping others to hone their own natural skills and love of knowledge.

Although an Investigator can become frustrated and impatient when their high levels of energy outmatch those of their students, learning to cultivate their patience and focus their nerves can help the Investigator be more productive, efficient, and compassionate.

Suggestions:
Converse with a trusted friend or colleague. Relax with video, board, or card games with others. Engage in group therapy. Mentor, volunteer, tutor, or lead a group. Engage in exercise – especially with a group. Practice learning physical and practical skills to see yourself as a learner while also directly connecting with people who are experts in non-intellectual areas.

There are simple things an Investigator can do to release their deep understanding of ideas and concepts into practical, useful ways for others, especially when they give themselves permission to be vulnerable.

Chapter Seven:
Ennea-Type Six –
"The Loyalist"

Aliases: The Devil's Advocate, The Questioner
The Committed, Security-Oriented type

Generally described as:

Engaging	*Responsible*
High-strung	*Intuitive*

At their best, Type Sixes are described as:

Skeptical	*Committed*
Self-Reliant	*Humorous*

Motto: "The world is a dangerous place. If I avoid making mistakes, I will be safe."

The Loyalist in General

People who exhibit a Core Type Six have a strong desire to live in a "safe" world, and actively work to create a secure environment through relationships and alliances. They place a high priority on duty, while also determining they should choose their own alliances and duties. Type Six people genuinely desire to defend and protect others, while also being afraid they can't defend and protect themselves.

They are often ambivalent toward authorities, indecisive about big ideas, and seemingly idiosyncratic to others. It is often said about Type Six people that "the opposite is also true." They are a bundle of contradictions.

When a Type Six person can fully engage and express themselves, they become confident leaders, reliable and supportive, tender and empathetic. They enjoy building a group of people who come together and cooperate for a cause. They make excellent team members and project coordinators, as it is naturally easy for them to be organized, proactive, and efficient decision makers.

Sometimes, while a Type Six person is working to develop a sense of security, they become overly cautious and indecisive when they experience anxiety about the "right" thing to do. When they doubt themselves, they also doubt others, which can lead to suspicious, judgmental treatment toward people they don't know and even those they do. Loyalists prefer to be seen as problem solvers, hard workers, and socially adaptable.

When a Type Six person develops a sense of dependability in their world, and trust in their inner guidance and emotions, they feel fulfilled. Their natural drive to feel secure means they create this security for others, becoming the go-to person when something needs to get done. Protecting and providing for others makes a Loyalist feel worthwhile.

How Loyalists See Themselves vs. How Others See Them

Loyalists see themselves as genuinely dedicated to working hard, but they also become resentful that they do too much, or fearful that they're not doing enough. They think they are driven by a true desire to make others feel accepted – truly loyal people – but actually, Loyalists generally operate under the feeling that no one accepts them. They often seek reassurance that they "are enough" and that others won't leave them at the first mistake. While the Loyalist believes that their intelligence makes them more in-tune with their emotions, other people may see the same intelligence as lacking emotion.

Loyalists are highly invested in seeing themselves as the "best" planners. They worry, thinking through issues they believe no one else does, seeing their anxieties as uncommon and perhaps shameful. They think others may not recognize it, but the drive to secure their world causes Type Sixes to become aggressive and angry.

Because Type Sixes are such deep thinkers, they often doubt their own ideas and decisions, which can make them heavily reliant on other people's opinions. Seeking out feedback, they may simultaneously also doubt it, and can even suspect that people are attempting to undermine them with bad advice. With too much reinforcement of this pattern, the Type Six begins to criticize, doubt, and rebuke all opinions from others.

While the Loyalist Ennea-type can see themselves as the embodiment of a mighty, protective warrior – because, in their view, they work hard to make the word better – they can come across as cowardly and paranoid at times. The Loyalist sees themselves as cooperative, while actually preventing group cohesion by being petty or manipulative when their emotions are not being addressed. While Type Sixes may enjoy or find fulfillment in having large networks that recognize their accomplishments, it can be frustrating to others when they begin to see their network's opinions as greater than their own.

The "Average" Loyalist's Mental Health

When Loyalists are at an average level of health, they may feel that they need to organize and make better decisions to bring the security that they seek into their lives. They are detail-oriented and vigilant, but also become demanding and cautious. Sometimes sending mixed messages to others about their needs, decisions can shift with new information. Loyalists at this level of health tend to exhibit passive-aggressive behaviors toward situations that threaten their security, while also priding themselves on being proactive toward problems and able to maintain many relationships at once.

When a Loyalist is feeling better than average, they may be full of the energy to organize, plan, and execute on their goals. They anticipate problems and can help others clearly see solutions to tough situations. At this level of health, a Loyalist wants everyone to see them as reliable and is quick to hand out favors and assistance, but they may also be sensitive, sarcastic, or argumentative.

Moving Toward Integration: Loyalists At Their Best

When moving in their Direction of Integration (growth) and exhibiting their best qualities, Loyalists become accepting, supportive, dutiful, and optimistic and can shed their fear.

> **Basic Desire(s):** To achieve security and support.
> **Basic Motivation(s):** To feel certain and sure, seeks security and support through others, even while testing the bounds of that support.
> **Unique Gift(s):** Warmth, loyalty, imagination, sense of humor.

Basic Goal: To achieve security through careful observation and alertness.

When Loyalist's Mental Health is Excellent

When at their best, Loyalists are trusting and trustworthy, selfless and courageous, optimistic and expressive. They both inspire and lead others, as they realize their interdependence with those in their close circles. Empathetic, intuitive, and thoughtful, they embody self-reliance and self-esteem.

As Type Six people Disintegrate, they become more selfish, less trusting, and less compassionate. Turning inward when they feel their safety is threatened, they begin to question bonds with others and to disconnect from anyone questionable. Although they enjoy and find fulfillment in working with others through positive relationships, they quickly divert energies into the relationships they see as most valuable.

Moving Toward Disintegration: Loyalists When Stressed

When moving in the Direction of Disintegration (stress), the normally relaxed and humorous Loyalist regresses toward becoming competitive and arrogant.

Basic Fear(s): Fears insecurity and anxiety, being alone and/or without guidance

Triggering Emotion(s): Fear and Doubt

When Fixated: Becomes cowardly

What Type Six People Might Struggle With

Type Six people can suffer from emotional disconnect and isolation, anxiety that causes them to obsess over small details that ends up pushing people away.

At times, Type Sixes can become so emotionally insecure that they become afraid of everything – "afraid of being afraid." The changing nature of the world can become overwhelming, and they may become paralyzed, preventing from making decisions, connecting with their emotions, and connecting with others. A Type Six person might spend time and energy focusing on the "chaos" and social "disruptions," ignoring the sense of peace they get from their relationships and established place in the world.

Type Sixes tend to overlook or ignore positive feelings and beliefs when under stress and dealing with challenge. Feelings of incompetence, unpreparedness, and disconnect from others can complicate their intense need security.

When Loyalist's Mental Health is Struggling

When fully disintegrated and under stress, Loyalists become paranoid and can lash out, feeling they need to protect themselves from everyone. They can suffer from high anxiety, paranoia, and self-destructive behavior, trying to keep themselves safe by cutting off society.

As Loyalists begin to decrease their stress and focus on higher levels of health, they become welcoming and trusting as they understand that not everyone is "out to get" them. The healthier the Loyalist's mindset, the less they will focus on the need to trust others and focus on the trust that people have already earned from them.

Potential Addictive Struggles

Type Six people might struggle with violent tendencies, "lashing out" at themselves or others when their security is threatened. In some cases, extreme feelings of stress or isolation can contribute to high levels of alcohol abuse, or use of caffeine and other stimulants.

Some Type Sixes may struggle with rigid ideas that impede their health, such as poor nutrition or excessive exercise habits. In order to achieve a feeling of stability, an unhealthy Type Six person may engage in intense levels of self-control with food, substances, or physical requirements.

Overcoming Challenges of the Loyalist Ennea-Type

It's important for the Loyalist to alleviate their anxiety. They feel things deeply, and being so intensely intellectual, can focus on their anxiety, feeling like it's higher than other people's. Which, in turn, increases their anxiety. If a Type Six personality is not working to trust and connect with others, they can become lost in their own fears. Healthy stress relief is essential for the Loyalist to stay balanced and at their best.

Being the Best Loyalist

Harness the best aspects of your Loyalist Ennea-type and diminish negative traits that emerge under stress. If you're a Loyalist, or know someone who is, consider how the following techniques can help you unlock and grow the best version of yourself.

Get Your Emotions Out

Type Six people need to embrace, explore, and come to terms with their anxieties. Sometimes, they can't recognize how their fearful energy can be focused to drive productivity and let them create amazing things. To maintain balance, a Loyalist should learn to listen, hear, and remember others' compliments and positive feedback. Anxiety can grow when they feel isolated, and when they feel they can't trust anyone, they will begin to doubt their own worth even more.

Type Six people find joy in finding a passion to pour their fears and anxieties into – something that they can engage in without judgment, or when the creation is shared, people they trust will support their efforts. By focusing on awareness of their emotional states, they will not be as subject to them, and will be able to maintain more balanced moods and healthier relationships.

Suggestions:

Engage in individual or group therapy, especially those that teach anxiety management and trust-building techniques. Meditate. Paint. Sculpt. Journal. Dance. Go to or perform in stand-up comedy or improv comedy. Exercise (in moderation), especially on a cooperative team.

Establish Peace and Order

Type Six people thrive when their environment supports low levels of anxiety. They are prone to clear, minimal, organized beauty, and when the world feels chaotic, it can reflect in their day-to-day lives. To maintain balance, a Loyalist must learn to be aware and manage their emotions, in their environment as well as their mind.

Type Six people find joy in appreciating the orderly beauty in the world, especially if they can integrate that order into their own lives. Trusting their own instincts and decisions for creating their world can teach them to actively engage with their agency in the world.

Suggestions:
Garden. Schedule regular deep cleaning projects around your home, with your car or bikes, and other often-used items that benefit from regular care. Organize a bookshelf, digital music collection, or other archive. Spend time at a library, aquarium, or museum. Take up a creative, hands-on detail-oriented hobby such as model building, digital photography editing, or knitting.

There are simple things a Loyalist can do to hone their ability to connect with others and their society at large, enhancing their own positivity, especially when they give themselves the freedom to trust their inner peace.

Chapter Eight:
Ennea-Type Seven –
"The Enthusiast"

Aliases: The Dreamer, The Doer
The Busy, Fun-Loving type

Generally described as:

Spontaneous	*Exciting*
Versatile	*High-Energy*

At their best, Type Sevens are described as:

Talented	*Driven*
Joyous	*Generous*

Motto: "Be happy and open to everything. More is better!"

The Enthusiast in General

People who exhibit a Core Type Seven have a strong desire to live life to the fullest, and actively work to avoid boredom for themselves and others. They place a priority on excitement, while also having so many interests that they spread themselves thin. Type Seven people genuinely enjoy others' company, while also being afraid they can never "do it all."

They are often impatient and impulsive, chasing whatever catches their attention. Bold and lively, they can be relentless in their pursuit of new and incredible experiences.

When a Type Seven person can fully engage and express themselves, they become optimistic, adventurous, and supportive of those around them. They enjoy using their energy to be productive but can have difficulty carrying a project through to completion. They make excellent guides, as they naturally learn from every experience and create a plan to make the next experience better.

Sometimes, when a Type Seven person is invested in an exciting project, they can demand others "keep up the pace" and maintain the same high levels of energy. They can feel such a selfishly pleasurable rush that they overlook the reactions of others. When they become bored, they get restless and can let their imaginations run wild. Enthusiasts prefer to be seen as intelligent, reliable, and most of all, fun.

When a Type Seven person develops a sense of supportive connections with others, where they can inspire and be engaged, they feel fulfilled. Their natural drive to make the most of life means that they see opportunities everywhere, both for themselves and for others. Laughing and creating valuable memories for others makes an Enthusiast feel worthwhile.

How Enthusiasts See Themselves vs. How Others See Them

Enthusiasts see themselves as genuinely productive and hard-working, but they can seem restless and unfocused to others. They think they are driven by a true desire to "experience it all" but actually, Enthusiasts generally operate from deep indecision or unsurety about what they really want. They often seek reassurance that they've made the "right choice" by trying to make "all the choices." While the Enthusiast believes that their intelligence helps them be more discerning, others can see the Enthusiast as disregarding their intellect to make decisions based on whimsy and emotion.

Enthusiasts are highly invested in enjoying life and especially, sharing joyful experiences with others. Their minds move quickly from one topic to another, sometimes leaving others too far behind to catch up. If they become disconnected from fun, they can begin to act out or take risks to create a sense of excitement in their life.

Because Type Sevens are intelligent without being intellectual, they don't tend to reflect on their emotions, which can put them out of touch with their true desires. When this happens, they may focus on things they "need" to do, making them focused on productivity and critical of their "failures." When this happens too much, the Enthusiast can begin to funnel their high energy into their emotions, becoming moody and unpredictable.

While the Enthusiast Ennea-type can see themselves as the embodiment of a "good time," because in their world view, they have tried it all and can give an educated opinion, they can come across as pushy or demanding. The Enthusiast sees themselves as the "life of the party," and they often can be, but when feeling insecure and anxious, they can drag a party down rather than lift it up.

The "Average" Enthusiast's Mental Health

When Enthusiasts are at an average level of health they may feel energized, unable to say "no", and uninhibited. They are ready to move and to avoid boredom, which can make them "up for anything." Sometimes restless, they can be unfocused or indecisive, as their high energy drives them to "do it all." Enthusiasts at this level of health tend to throw themselves into many activities, attracted to whatever presents itself as interesting or exciting.

When an Enthusiast is feeling better than average, they can be sophisticated and charming. Keeping up with the latest trends, they can be a source of information and fun for others, bringing new experiences to their social circle. At this level of health, Enthusiasts want everyone to have fun, and to see them as fun, but they may also be insatiable in their search and demanding that others keep up with them.

Moving Toward Integration: Enthusiasts At Their Best

When moving in their Direction of Integration (growth) and exhibiting their best qualities, Enthusiasts become focused and joyful and shed their greed for experience.

> **Basic Desire(s):** To be satisfied, to "live a full life"
>
> **Basic Motivation(s):** To enjoy the maximum worthwhile experiences, to capitalize on every moment and passion, to experience freedom and happiness
>
> **Unique Gift(s):** Playful, inspiring, creative, optimistic, passionate, extroverted.
>
> **Basic Goal:** To experience joy now and in the future.

When Enthusiast's Mental Health is Excellent

When at their best, Enthusiasts are deeply grateful for life, focused on bounty and joy, resilient and extroverted. They both lead and support others, as they enjoy their own successes and those of their group. Vivacious, charming, spontaneous, and responsive to others' needs, Enthusiasts at their best embody a "carpe diem" mentality.

As Type Seven people Disintegrate, they become more self-centered, perfectionistic, and focused on negative emotions. Turning away from the "extras" in life, they become critical of the simple things, feeling dissatisfied with themselves and others. Although they find fulfillment in being productive and useful, they become more conservative with their energy and less likely to push themselves to achieve.

Moving Toward Disintegration: Enthusiasts When Stressed

When moving in the Direction of Disintegration (stress), the normally upbeat Enthusiast regresses toward becoming critical, greedy, and scattered.

> **Basic Fear(s):** Fear of missing out, deprivation, and pain
> **Triggering Emotion(s):** Greed, gluttony.
> **When Fixated:** Becomes rigid and inflexible.

What Type Seven People Might Struggle With

Type Seven people can suffer from high expectations of themselves or others, creating obsessive tendencies and anxiety.

At times, Type Sevens can become so deeply afraid that they aren't "making the most" of their lives, that they push themselves past reasonable physical and emotional capacities. They may overschedule themselves, eat and drink too much in an attempt to try every option, or push themselves not only to meet a deadline but to submit a "perfect" project by the deadline. A Type Seven person might spend time and energy focusing on including "everything," ignoring the argument that more is not always better.

Type Sevens tend to overlook their true emotions and ideas in their focus on the excitement of the outside world. Boredom, dissatisfaction, and disappointment can complicate their high drive to do, see, say, and live "fully."

When Enthusiast's Mental Health is Struggling

When fully disintegrated and under stress, Enthusiasts become impulsive and needy. Selfish and self-centered, they become panicky as they spiral in anxiety. They can become self-destructive or abusive, as they struggle to deal with intense emotions and a need to elicit strong emotions from others.

As Enthusiasts begin to decrease their stress and focus on higher levels of health, they become more focused and dedicated to relationships and passion projects. The healthier the Enthusiast's mindset, the less they will "act out" for attention, instead relying on their genuine intelligence to fuel their high energy levels toward healthy outlets.

Potential Addictive Struggles

Type Seven people might struggle with addictions to substances that give them "heightened" or new experiences – narcotics, alcohol, stimulants, and hallucinogens. In some cases, extreme feelings of rejection can contribute to the drive to "keep up with" others in their substance use.

Some Type Sevens might struggle with the physical expectations they place on their bodies. They may seek cosmetic surgeries or overexert themselves in exercise programs. In order to achieve a feeling of worth, they may engage in enthusiastically promoting these unhealthy activities to others.

Overcoming Challenges of the Enthusiast Ennea-Type

It's important for the Enthusiast to be allowed to explore. Focused on joy, they need to allow themselves to experience their entire emotional range, without fear of rejection or isolation from others. After a short period reflecting on other feelings, the Enthusiast can feel more connected to their gratitude. If a Type Seven person is not working to enjoy the moment, they will become focused on future joy and can experience more poignant disappointment when the joy doesn't meet their high expectations. Healthy reflection and support from others are essential for the Enthusiast to stay balanced and at their best.

Being the Best Enthusiast

Harness the best aspects of your Enthusiast Ennea-type and diminish negative traits that emerge under stress. If you're an Enthusiast, or know someone who is, consider how using these techniques can help you unlock and grow the best version of yourself.

Turn Impulses into Plans

Type Seven people need to explore the world. Sometimes, they can't recognize how their relentless pursuit doesn't leave enough room for as many quality experiences as possible. To maintain balance, an Enthusiast should learn to curb their impulses, focusing their energy to formulate wishes and dreams into plans. By channeling great ideas into actionable lists, Enthusiasts not only harness their imagination but exhibit the best of their productivity skills.

Type Seven people find joy in involving others in their fun. By learning to cooperatively plan new, fun experiences with others, Enthusiasts can develop patience and experience not only their own joy, but the shared joy of others.

Suggestions:
Use lists to organize tasks and ideas. Learn to delay impulses by saving the idea and revisiting it another day. Paint. Join a performance group. Journal about all emotions. Join a group sport or exercise league. Consider investing or financial planning.

Let Others Guide You
Type Seven people thrive when they are open to learning from others, including nature, their environment, and historical figures. They can lower their anxiety when being guided through a new experience, and often benefit from taking suggestions from others. To maintain balance, an Enthusiast must learn to follow others not only to places that seem

exciting, places with high energy activities, but also when they explore places of quiet, peace, and connection with themselves.

Type Seven people find joy in *doing things* not in being *distracted*, although they can become distractable when unfocused. Learning to focus on long-term goals and pacing their energy can teach them to be even-tempered and empathetic.

Suggestions:

Meditate. Take lessons in an artform or sport. Practice yoga. Volunteer, mentor, or tutor. Spend time with children, elders, and animals. Study spirituality and reflect on deep meanings of your experiences. Confide in a trustworthy, nonjudgmental companion. Group therapy can inspire new interests and personal connections.

Enthusiasts can do simple things to embrace and live out their excitement for life, especially when they give themselves permission to embrace others and their energy.

Chapter Nine:
Type Eight –
"The Challenger"

Aliases: The Boss, The Leader
The Powerful, Dominating type

Generally described as:

Confident	*Decisive*
Willful	*Tenacious*

At their best, Type Eights are described as:

Assertive	*Masterful*
Heroic	*Reliable*

Motto: "I must be strong. It's my way or the highway"

The Challenger in General

People who exhibit a Core Type Eight have a strong desire to create safety in their world, and actively work to harness their inner strength for the benefit of the people they care about. They place priority on power as a route to safety, which can lead to fear of dependency or weakness. Type Eight people genuinely desire to protect and serve others, while also being afraid they won't be capable.

They are often inspiring with their assertive, confident nature, which contributes to Challengers being natural leaders. Resourceful and creative, they can be cunning and vengeful when they feel vulnerable or that they've been "wronged" by another.

When a Type Eight person is working toward a goal, they can become domineering in their attempt to eliminate uncertainty and control their environment. Challenging and confrontational, they jump at opportunities with wholehearted dedication. When afraid, their charm can turn to emotional abuse, exposing and belittling others at their weak points. However, Challengers prefer to be seen as valuable, tough, and impenetrable sources of strength for others.

When a Type Eight person can fully engage and express themselves, they become beacons of independence, inspiring others to achieve great things. They enjoy building a sense of security, even separating themselves from social conventions to create a world of their own standards. They make excellent public servants and leaders, motivating others to question their own strengths and push through their weaknesses.

How Challengers See Themselves vs. How Others See Them

Challengers see themselves as genuinely resistant to weakness, but they also are incredibly fearful of being weak or seen as weak. They think they are driven by a true desire to create a better world for everyone – strong for the sake of others – but actually, Challengers generally operate under a sense of inadequacy and determination to prove themselves otherwise. They often seek reassurance from others through domination – if others submit, it must prove they are strong, without recognizing that fear is not the only source of strength. While the Challenger believes that they should have the agency to accept and reject the value of people and things in their world, they may come across as judgmental and mercilessly dominating.

Challengers are invested in seeing themselves as industrious and productive, protective and selfless, and can become hurt when others don't recognize their strength or focus on the weaknesses they work hard to conceal. Although they believe there is no reason for anyone to reject them, they are desperate for others' acceptance and recognition.

Because Type Eights fear being misunderstood, they are prone to suppressing and hiding their emotions. Seeking out validation for their ideas of themselves, they may reject others before others have the chance to reject them. With too much of this behavior, they can become argumentative, confrontational, and toxic to their own relationships.

While the Challenger Ennea-type can see themselves as the embodiment of practical, common-sense decision making and righteous protectors – because, in their view, they work hard to stay positive and "fight for what's right" – they can come across as detached, insensitive, and overbearing. The Challenger sees themselves as a protector of their world's security, which can lead them to disregard others' desires and needs, and although they are working to "keep everyone safe," they may lose sight of what it takes to make others happy.

The "Average" Challenger's Mental Health

When Challengers are at an average level of health, they may feel strong in their environment, capable of leading others. Proud and high-energy, they can become domineering and overbearing. Ruggedly resourceful, they can sometimes push people away with their individualism. Challengers at this level of health tend to exhibit some risk taking and self-centered behaviors that threaten their connections with others, as they can be intimidating without meaning to.

When a Challenger is feeling better than average, they are hard-working and dedicated. They don't let things stand in the way of their goals and will push others to have the same commitment to their own dreams. They are practical, problem-solvers, and may have a bold disregard for societal norms or even laws. At this level of health, the Challenger wants everyone to see their ideas and opinions and "best" and "worthy" of being followed.

Moving Toward Integration: Challengers At Their Best

When moving in their Direction of Integration (growth) and exhibiting their best qualities, Challengers become warm and caring, and are able to shed their need to control.

Basic Desire(s): To control their destiny

Basic Motivation(s): To prove strength and resiliency through self-reliance.

Unique Gift(s): Brave, powerful, straightforward, protector of the weak.

Basic Goal: To harness strength through control.

When Challenger's Mental Health is Excellent

When at their best, Challengers are masters of goal-achievement, pushing the boundaries of potential into the realms of reality. Truly heroic leaders, they are generous and committed to the betterment of the group, even to the point of putting themselves in danger for the "right reasons." Authoritative, decisive, and helpful, they embody confidence and perseverance.

As Type Eight people Disintegrate, they become argumentative, belligerent, or insensitive to others' feelings and ideas. While they think they are "standing up" for what they want, they can actually be knocking down or mowing over others' desires and needs. Although they find fulfillment in championing others, they can also become protective and competitive against people outside, or even inside, their trusted circles.

Moving Toward Disintegration: Challengers When Stressed

When moving in the Direction of Disintegration (stress), the normally supportive and confident Challenger regresses toward becoming fearful and possessive.

Basic Fear(s): Being controlled and harmed by others.
Triggering Emotion(s): Lust
When Fixated: Becomes vengeful

What Type Eight People Might Struggle With

Type Eight people can suffer from anger and stress management, becoming anxious and lashing out when their security is threatened.

At times, Type Eights can become so emotionally invested in the safety of the world that they become paranoid or delusional about real fears or dangers, instead focusing on things that frighten or upset them but not others. A Type Eight person might spend time and energy working to build a "safe" world, while disregarding others' sense of security and imposing their ideas and will onto others' lives.

Type Eights tend to overlook their own accomplishments, always driven to "do more" when stressed. They may react to feelings of vulnerability by becoming possessive, obsessive, and self-righteous.

When Challenger's Mental Health is Struggling

When fully disintegrated and under stress, Challengers become controlling, merciless, and manipulative. They can suffer from anxieties related to losing their sense of control, and develop delusions and paranoia. Some Challengers develop a sense of invincibility, with others regress to a state of helplessness, but either emotional reaction can result in a stubborn denial of others' attempts to influence them.

As Challengers decrease their stress and focus on higher levels of health, they become more inclusive, less destructive, and more cognizant of their effects on others. The healthier the Challenger's mentality, the less they focus on using their strength *against* others and the more they focus on using that strength *for* others.

Potential Addictive Struggles

Type Eight people might struggle with violent tendencies, anti-social behaviors, or control issues. In some cases, extreme feelings of being "unstoppable" can lead them to immoral or illegal actions, without regard for their own safety.

Some Type Eights may struggle with self-harm, including addictions to alcohol, narcotics, tobacco, or exercise programs. They may control themselves through food or self-abuse, and can avoid medical checkups to avoid discussing their physical symptoms with others.

Overcoming Challenges of the Challenger Ennea-Type

It's important for the Challenger to let go of their need to control. They experience deep emotions that often frighten them with their intensity and speed, which can cause them to experience a "flight or fight" reaction to their own moods. If a

Type Eight personality is not working to understand what frightens them, they can become lost in a fight against themselves. Stress release and acceptance from their community are essential for the Challenger to stay balanced and at their best.

Being the Best Challenger

Harness the best aspects of your Challenger Ennea-type and diminish negative traits that emerge under stress. If you're a Challenger, or know someone who is, the following techniques can help you unlock and grow the best version of yourself.

Practice Generosity and Gratitude

Type Eight people need to feel valuable to others. Sometimes, they strive for this value through power, but they must work to recognize the value that comes from giving to others. To maintain balance, a Challenger should learn to *give their power* to others – whether through charitable contributions, distributing their time and knowledge, and sharing their thanks to everyone who has supported them in their efforts to create security.

Type Eight people find joy in acceptance and recognition from others, especially when they are recognized for leadership and innovation. By focusing on praising and lifting up others, they accumulate a sense of security through others' respect and admiration.

Suggestions:

Volunteer, mentor, or tutor. End every conversation and interaction with "thank you." Schedule cards, gifts, and well-wishes to people you care about. Engage in group therapy, especially those that teach anxiety management and trust-building techniques. Journal, paint, sculpt, or dance to physically and mentally explore emotions in a safe space.

Cultivate Restraint and Compassion

Type Eight people struggle learning to yield to others and can benefit from cultivating their empathy. They are prone to quick, decisive action, and learning to slow down and submit can present them with challenges that inspire them to grow and demonstrate the value of being a follower as well as a leader. To maintain balance, a Challenger can learn to set their ego aside and learn from watching others protect themselves.

Type Eight people find joy in watching others grow, which means they have to sometimes restrain themselves from taking control over every situation. Learning to trust and care for other people as individuals (and not possessions) teaches them to respect the needs and agency of others.

Suggestions:

Be an audience participant in a live arts or sports venue – purchase season tickets and frequent the performances or games, to passively appreciate and support growth of others in their accomplishments. Become a sponsor or subscriber to local organizations – not a board member or important figure, but a guest, visitor, or patron. Practice active listening without solving others' problems or taking on their burdens.

There are simple things a Challenger can do to hone their ability to submit and connect with others, and to open up emotionally, especially when they give themselves permission to enjoy the world and people in it as they are.

Chapter Ten:
Ennea-Type Nine –
"The Peacemaker"

Aliases: The Mediator, The Spiritual-Minded
The Easygoing, Self-Sacrificing type

Generally described as:

Accepting	*Supportive*
Agreeable	*Complacent*

At their best, Type Nines are described as:

All-Embracing	*Diplomatic*
Healers	*Even-Tempered*

Motto: "Why get upset about things you can't change? I am at peace"

The Peacemaker in General

People who exhibit a Core Type Nine have a strong desire to connect with people, their environment, and the universe at large. They place a priority on harmony, belonging, and keeping traditions and deep values present in day-to-day life.

Type Nine people genuine desire to make the world a better place, while also being afraid that they don't have a strong sense of their own identity.

They seek acceptance and comfort in others, sometimes blending and confusing their personal desires with those of the group. Nurturing and receptive, Type Nine people can also become passive to a point of complacency.

When a Type Nine person can fully engage and express themselves, they devote themselves to great ideals such as truth, love, and beauty. Often deeply spiritual, they work to live out their philosophies, which can cause them to struggle with the realities of the chaotic, conflict-driven world around them. Tension can paralyze them into indecision or apathy, as they turn inward in a search for meaningful identity. They make excellent advisors, teachers, and social servants, inspiring others with their natural abilities to mediate and resolve conflict.

Type Nine people can focus so intently on the needs and energies of those in their group that they become disconnected from their own desires. When they feel cut off from their inner source, they can become static, stagnant, and stubborn to change. Peacemakers prefer to be seen as figures of movement and resolution, like flowing water that washes away pain and problems.

When a Type Nine person develops a sense of security in their group, their identity is reinforced and their efforts are appreciated, they feel fulfilled. Their natural drive to make the world "better" means they need to see themselves integrated in that better world. Positive influence on others makes a Peacemaker feel worthwhile.

How Peacemakers See Themselves vs. How Others See Them

Peacemakers see themselves as genuinely centered and openminded, but they also become anxious about losing their true identity. They think they are driven by a true desire to make others happy and to be a calming presence, but actually Peacemakers generally operate under fear of being incompetent when presented with a problem. They often seek reassurance from others that they have the "right view" or the "best solution," while subconsciously creating the tension they attempt to avoid.

Peacemakers are highly invested in seeing themselves as calm under pressure, empathetic to all points of view, adaptable and diplomatic. They think others may not recognize it, but the drive to make others happy can often cause them to forget their own happiness. When not truly devoted in their energies, their efforts become lackluster.

Because Type Nines are so deeply emotional, they can invest those emotions in many things outside themselves, leaving little compassion or understanding for their own struggles against failure. Seeking out acceptance from others, they can forget to be accepting. With too much reinforcement, they can become passive and apathetic toward the positivity they receive from others. Or, they can exhibit "toxic positivity" – exhibiting an almost-delusional focus on the "silver lining" of every situation, refusing to acknowledge or address any negativity.

The "Average" Peacemaker's Mental Health

When Peacemakers are at an average level of health, they may feel connected with reality and others in their world. It can be easy for them to be compliant and helpful, even to the point of disregarding their own wants and needs. Accommodating to the point of being passive, they may begin to feel pressure from doing things they aren't truly invested in, which can make them unfocused and complacent. Peacemakers at this level of health can exhibit some passive-aggressive tendencies, as they work to maintain positive connections with others, even in conflict of their own desires.

When a Peacemaker feels better than average, they may be charged with energy to resolve and work through conflicts. As they take up their expected roles, they find it easy to navigate the emotional pressures of others and find solutions that satisfy everyone. Spiritual and philosophical, Peacemakers see the good in others and seamlessly can dedicate themselves to "clearing a path" for other people to succeed.

Moving Toward Integration: Peacemakers At Their Best

When moving in their Direction of Integration (growth) and exhibiting their best qualities, Peacemakers become accepting and energetic and can shed their worries.

> **Basic Desire(s):** To achieve "peace of mind" and inner stability
>
> **Basic Motivation(s):** To create harmony, avoid conflict, preserve positive emotions, and resist negativity.
>
> **Unique Gift(s):** Nonjudgmental, accepting, empathetic, intuitive.
>
> **Basic Goal:** To establish peace through understanding and connectivity.

When Peacemaker's Mental Health is Excellent

When at their best, Peacemakers are content with themselves and the world around them. They feel connected to the best of the universe and can provide others profound insight into new ideas and their own potential. Present in the moment, joyful of new experience, they are supportive and generous, good-natured and patient.

As Type Nine people Disintegrate, they become more self-conscious and less serene. Turning inward to seek the peace they aren't finding with connections in the world, they begin to focus on problems and complexities rather than solutions. Although they enjoy trusting and relying on others, they can lose sense of their own identity and come to mistrust their intuition and rely on the group to define them.

Moving Toward Disintegration: Peacemakers When Stressed

When moving in their Direction of Disintegration (stress), the normally open-minded and easygoing Peacemaker regresses toward becoming anxious and self-neglecting.

> **Basic Fear(s):** Fears loss and separation
> **Triggering Emotion(s):** Laziness, sloth
> **When Fixated:** Becomes apathetic, lackluster

What Type Nine People Might Struggle With

Type Nine people can suffer from depression and anxiety, created by insecurity around their identity and connections to the world.

At times, Type Nines can become so emotionally broken down that they attempt to block out tension and pain by numbing themselves to outside influence. They then lose touch with their true needs and become lost in a sense of purposelessness and inadequacy. A Type Nine person might spend time and energy toward solving problems with overly complicated solutions, pushing people away as they passive-aggressively seek acceptance from others.

Type Nines tend to overlook or ignore their needs and emotions when involved in a group and feel disconnected from inner peace when disconnected from a group. Feelings of deep love and commitment complicate their independent, peace-seeking nature.

When Peacemaker's Mental Health is Struggling

When fully disintegrated and under stress, Peacemakers become numb, demoralized, mere shells of themselves. They can suffer from depression, nihilism, and dependency on others to fill their emotional needs.

As Peacemakers decrease their stress and focus on higher levels of health, they become more aware of simple solutions and true positive emotions. The healthier the Peacemaker's mindset, the less they will be "frozen in place" and the more creative and easygoing they become.

Potential Addictive Struggles

Type Nine people might struggle with neglecting their own needs, including malnutrition and irregular medical checkups. They may repress their anger, focusing it inward, which can cause disconnect with others, loneliness, depression, and anxiety.

Some Type Nines may struggle with peer pressure and going along with the group, which can result in unhealthy diet or exercise habits, or use of addictive substances. In order to achieve a feeling of acceptance, Peacemakers may engage in self-harm or self-abasement.

Overcoming Challenges of the Peacemaker Ennea-Type

It's important for the Peacemaker to "be the change" in the world. They thrive with deep connections to others, especially in roles of conflict resolution where they don't have to be an authority, but instead they can be an advisor or guide. If a Type

Nine personality is not working toward creating harmony with others, they can get lost in a sense of chaos. Learning to trust their body and inner motivations are essential for the Peacemaker to stay balanced and at their best.

Being the Best Peacemaker

Harness the best aspects of your Peacemaker Ennea-type and diminish negative traits that emerge under stress. If you're a Peacemaker, or know someone who is, the following techniques can help you unlock and grow the best version of yourself.

Get Corporeal

Type Nine people need to embrace their physical and emotional needs. They can be so focused on the exterior that they neglect the interior, and becoming grounded within themselves can alleviate anxiety created from outside pressures. To maintain balance, a Peacemaker must learn to assert themselves – speak up in conversations, push their physical limits, offer their opinions and insight.

Type Nine people find joy in having their own "space" – mental, physical, and emotional. Although they do not want to be isolated and are happiest when their personal space shares intimate boundaries, or even overlaps, with the space of the group. By focusing on keeping some of their energy for themselves, their sense of balance can feed their support of others.

Suggestions:

Develop a workout routine – running, swimming, yoga, weightlifting, dance, etc. Learn to channel aggression and tension into activity. Walk in nature. Practice active listening and speaking up in group settings; group therapy can help with this. Journal. Draw or paint. Teach or mentor a physical activity to children.

Prioritize Relationships

Type Nine people need to love and be loved, accept and be accepted. Sometimes, they begin to focus on emotions, reactions, and relationships that will not support their long-term goals and happiness. To maintain balance, a Peacemaker can learn to prioritize the most valuable opinions and ideas in their life, streamlining their decision-making processes and keeping them connected with what truly matters to them.

Type Nine people find joy in watching others learn, love, and grow, and seek out joy in daily situations. They often struggle to accept or work through pain and must learn to confront and heal from conflicts and tensions. They can feel deep betrayal if they aren't allowed to express their joy for others, and they must work to restore harmony through self-appreciation and self-compassion.

Suggestions:

Engage in individual or group therapy. Prioritize expressing your emotions to significant others. Meditate, practice yoga, or engage in martial arts, especially with loved ones. Limit social media, television, and news exposure. Walk in, photograph, or connect with nature and animals. Cultivate a close social circle who you share every achievement, joy, and sorrow with.

Peacemakers can do simple things to hone their abilities to add value to the world, especially when they give themselves the benefit of learning to live with their anxieties.

Conclusion

Thank you again for purchasing this book!

I hope this book was able to help you to understand your Ennea-type and the Types of people in your life. I hope this knowledge allows you to grow, recognize your own potential, and overcome challenges that hold you back.

The next step is to act! I've provided suggestions and solutions to help you achieve the best version of yourself, depending on your Type. So now, all you have to do is find the solution that works for you and live a happier, fuller life.

I'm so glad you've made it to the end of this book, and I hope you've found some worth in it. If you would be so kind, I'd really appreciate it if you would leave a positive review and share your experience, so others might be able to find this book and start their learning.

Thank you and good luck!

References

"A Complete Mobile Enneagram Guide" By EnneaApp. 2019.
<https://enneaapp.com/>

"How the Enneagram System Works" By The Enneagram Institute®. 2017.
< https://www.enneagraminstitute.com/how-the-enneagram-system-works>

"How to Change Your Life Using the Enneagram – Part 2: Discover Your Type" By Bayside Church. *Medium*. 30 Dec. 2016.
<https://medium.com/@BaysideChurch/how-to-change-your-life-using-the-enneagram-part-2-discover-your-type-e78fcdd396c

"How to Use the Enneagram Personality for Personal Growth" By Rezzan Husssey. *The Art of Wellbeing*. 1 Nov. 2017.
<http://www.artofwellbeing.com/2017/11/01/enneagramofpersonality/>

"What's Your Type?" By Jean Kummerow. *TedxGrinnellCollege*. YouTube video. 3 Feb. 2017.
<https://www.youtube.com/watch?v=gBkIyJ7kf_I>

www.ingramcontent.com/pod-product-compliance
Lightning Source LLC
Chambersburg PA
CBHW020324290526
45785CB00007B/2914